THE GREAT BIG BOOK OF MIGHTY MACHINES

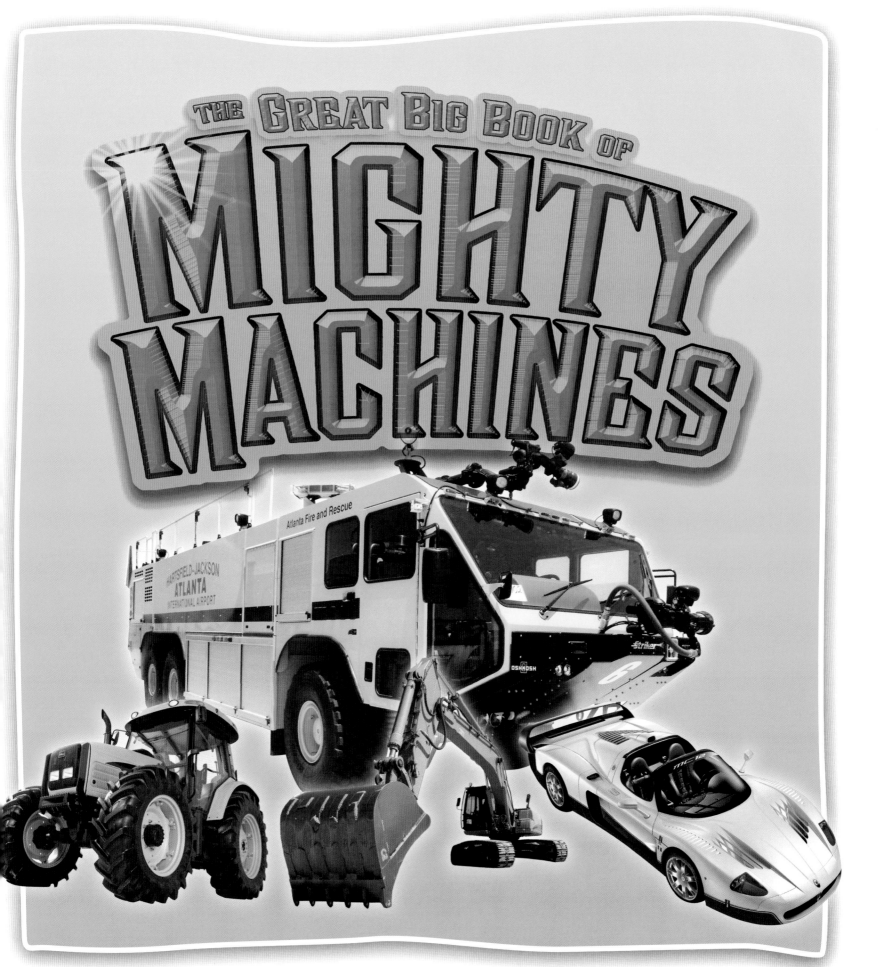

A FIREFLY BOOK

Published by Firefly Books Ltd. 2009
Copyright © QEB Publishing, Inc. 2008

Third Printing, 2016

Publisher Cataloging-in-Publication Data (U.S.)

Coppendale, Jean.
   The great big book of mighty machines / Jean Coppendale
[160] p. : col. photos. ; cm.
Includes index.
Summary: Information on various massive moving machines, including: monster trucks, dump trucks, fire trucks, tractors, big bikes, cranes, trains and airplanes.
ISBN: 978-1-55407-521-8
1. Machinery. I. Title.
621.805 dc22   QL467.C677 2009

Library and Archives Canada Cataloguing in Publication

Coppendale, Jean.
   The great big book of mighty machines / Jean Coppendale
[160] p. : col. photos. ; cm.
Includes index.
Summary: Information on various massive moving machines, including: monster trucks, dump trucks, fire trucks, tractors, big bikes, cranes, trains and airplanes.
ISBN: 978-1-55407-521-8
1. Machinery. I. Title.
621.805 dc22   QL467.C677 2009

Published in the United States by
Firefly Books (U.S.) Inc.
P.O. Box 1338, Ellicott Station
Buffalo, New York 14205

Published in Canada by
Firefly Books Ltd.
50 Staples Avenue, Unit 1
Richmond Hill, Ontario L4B 0A7

Printed and bound in China

Author Jean Coppendale and Ian Graham
Designers Phil and Traci Morash
Editor Paul Manning
Picture Researcher Claudia Tate

Publisher Steve Evans
Creative Director Zeta Davies
Managing Editor Amanda Askew

Picture credits
(t=top, b=bottom, c=center, l=left, r=right, FC=front cover)
Agripictures 77t
AGStockUSA Dave Reede 70–71, Mirek Weichsel 74–75, Dave Reede 78–79
Alamy Eric Nathan 18, Steve Hamblin 19, Gunter Marx 60–61, Peter Titmuss 61t, Justin Kase 109t, South West Images Scotland 123t
ALSTOM Transport 56–57
Artemis Images Pikes Peak Hill Climb 140
BMW 28, 38
CLAAS KGaA ltd 69t, 80–81
Clive Featherby 139t
Corbis Leo Mason 11, Marvy! 14, Richard H Cohen 22, Tim de Waele 23, Anthony West 26 bc, George Tiedemann/GT Images 36, Mazen Mahdi/epa 37t, David Cooper/Toronto Star/ZUMA 39t, Don Mason 40, Alex Hofford/epa 44, Brooks Kraft 45t, Paul A Souders 53t, Construction Photography 127, Richard T Nowitz 147, Transtock 148, Ross Pictures 151, Regis Duvignau 135t, Rick Fowler 150
Dave Toussaint Photography 54–55, 64–65
Denis Baldwin 58–59
Ford Motor Company 102–103
Frankish Enterprises 144b
Fred Guenther 62–63
Freightliner LLC 130–131
Getty Images 42, AFP/Oliver Lang 146, Tim de Frisco 137t
The Glacier Express 51t
GM UK & Ireland 33t
Hochtief Aktiengesellchaft 126b
Holt Studios 79t
J S Kaczanowski – Tuscola, Illinois USA 129t
JCB 112, 117t
Joe Osciak 48–49
Komatsu 120, 121
Louie Schoeman 52–53
New Holland 82–83
OEAMTC 101t
Oshkosh Truck Corporation 94–95, 100–101
Paul Lantz 11 b
Paul Mayall Photography 114–115
Photolibrary Jtb Photo Communications Inc 50–51, 63, Index Stock Imagery 74b, Photo Researchers Inc 89t, Mauritius Die Bildagentur Gmbh 90–91, Index Stock Imagery 96–97, Photo Researchers Inc 97t
Reuters Fabrizio Bensch 104b, Guido Benschop 104–105
Rex Features Justin Downing 142, 134, SIPA 136
Ridgeback 8
Royal Navy LA(Phot) Emma Somerfield 99t
SBB AG, Bern – Fotodienst/Alain D Boillat 49
Scania CV AB (publ) Dan Boman 115t
Shutterstock Cornel Achirei 9, Tom Richards 12, Keith Robinson 13, Maxim Petrichuk 15, Ravshan Mirzaitov 16, Lucian Coman 17, Maxim Petrichuk 20, Max Blain 21, Timothy Large 24, 25, Anthony Hall, 26br, Joseph Gareri 29t, Toyota (GB) PLC 30, Richard Foreman 31t, Julie Lucht 32, Anatoliy Meshkov 34, Maserati S.p.A. 35t, Mikolaj Tomczak 41t, Losevsky Pavel 43, Keith Levit 88–89, Micah May 91t, Mark William Penny 98–99, nialat 108, Zygalski Krzysztof 110, ownway 110b, Brad Whitsitt 111t, Ljupco Smokovski 116, Mark Atkins 118, Florin C 119t, Kamil Sobócki 122, Mark Atkins 124, Stanislav Komogorov 125a, Michael Stokes FC 138, Maksim Shmeljov 136, 141t, 143, Barry Salmons 145, Khafizov Ivan Harisovich 148
Steffen Schoner 128–129
Still Pictures BIOS Gunther Michel 92–93, Markus Dlouhy 93b, Jochen Tack 103t
Valtra 84–85
Volvo 113t

THE GREAT BIG BOOK OF MIGHTY MACHINES

Jean Coppendale and Ian Graham

FIREFLY BOOKS

Contents

Monster trucks

Words in **bold** can be
found in the glossary
on page 153.

Bikes

What is a cycle?

Cycles are a useful way to travel around. Bicycles have two wheels that move when the rider pushes down on the pedals. A motorcycle has an engine. It can go much faster than a pedal bike.

Pushing the pedals turns the back wheel and makes the bicycle move. Squeezing the brake handles makes the bicycle stop.

brake handles

pedal

There are all sorts of different motorcycles. Sports cycles and racing motorcycles are fast. **Trail** cycles are for riding off-road, on dirt tracks.

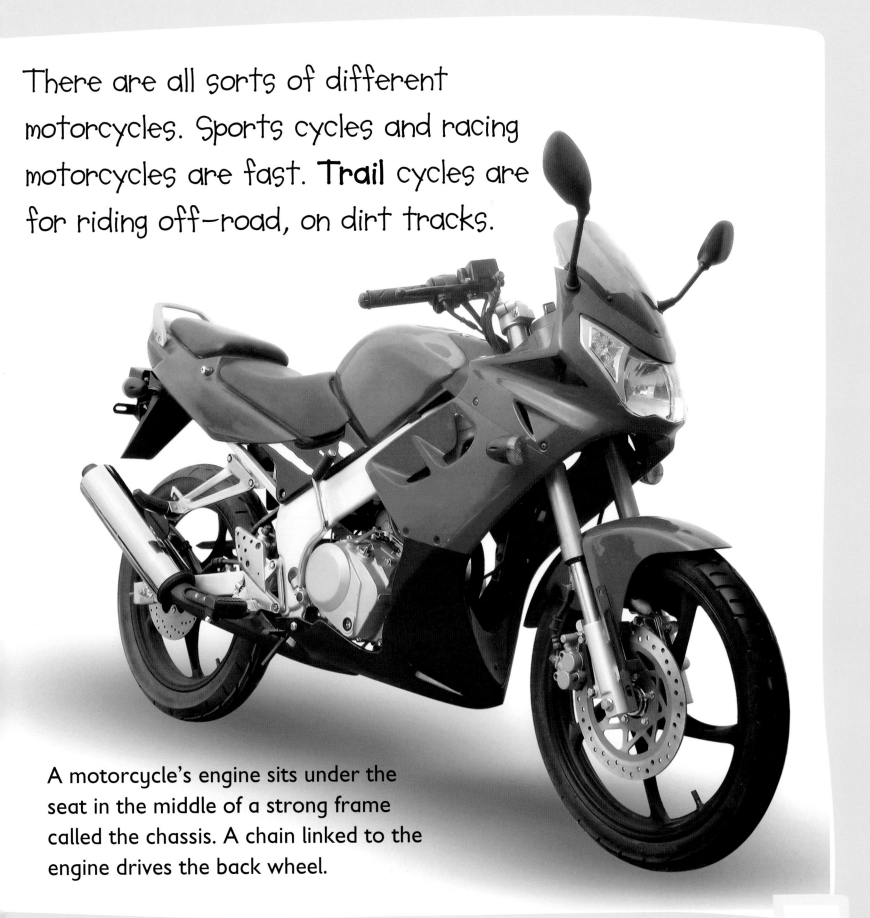

A motorcycle's engine sits under the seat in the middle of a strong frame called the chassis. A chain linked to the engine drives the back wheel.

Superbikes

A superbike is a light sports motorcycle with an incredibly powerful engine to give it extra zip. Superbikes are among the fastest cycles on the road.

Motorcycle racing is a really popular sport. Motorcycle races can be held on road tracks, special racing circuits or off-road.

To go around corners at speed, superbike riders lean over until they almost touch the ground.

Motocross

Motocross races are held on hilly dirt tracks full of **obstacles** and jumps. The motorcycles have special **tires** to grip the track.

Riders must think fast to work out the quickest way around the track. They need to be fit to take part, so they train hard.

Motocross riders jump high into the air on their cycle. They can be injured if they are thrown off the cycle at high speed.

Motocross cycles need good **suspension** and springy wheels to cushion them against bumps and jolts.

Easy riders

Harley-Davidsons are big, powerful motorcycles with lots of shiny **chrome**. They are heavy cycles, made for sitting back and cruising along the open road.

Some owners **customize** their cycles by adding extra chrome fittings and high handlebars. These cycles are sometimes called choppers, because their owners chop off the parts they do not need.

The Harley-Davidson's **exhaust** is famous for the deep, throaty roar it makes!

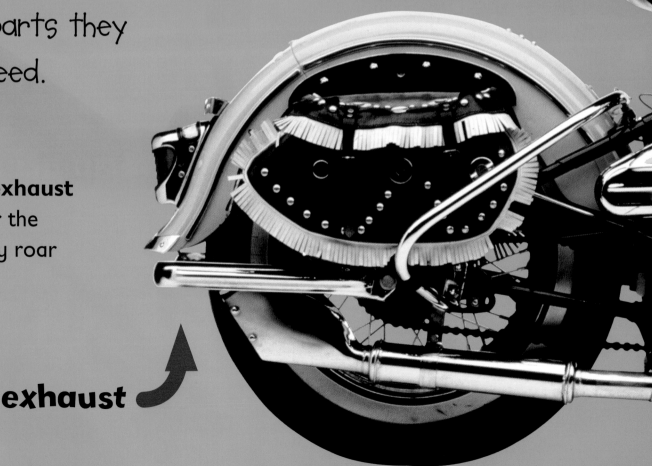

exhaust

14

Many police forces use Harley-Davidson motorcycles because they are fast, yet also good for weaving in and out of **traffic**.

Quad bikes

A quad bike is a motorcycle with four wide wheels. It is useful for moving across soft or muddy ground without getting stuck. Many farmers use quad bikes to get around their land.

At quad sports events, riders race their bikes over all kinds of ground, from snow and ice to beaches and sandy desert.

This farmer is using a quad bike to help round up a flock of sheep.

Most quad bikes have four-wheel drive. The engine drives all four wheels. This helps the wheels to keep a grip on rough or bumpy ground.

Scooters

For zipping through busy city traffic, nothing beats a scooter. It has a smaller engine and wheels than other types of motorcycles. Instead of sitting astride the cycle, riders place their feet on a footrest between the wheels.

A motorscooter taxi whisks passengers through the busy streets of Bangkok, Thailand.

A scooter is not as fast as a motorcycle, but it is good for short journeys around town.

In Italy, a scooter is the favorite way of getting around.

Off-road bikes

Mountain bikes are made for riding off-road on rough ground. Their frames have to be stronger than ordinary bikes to stand up to jolts and knocks without getting bent or twisted.

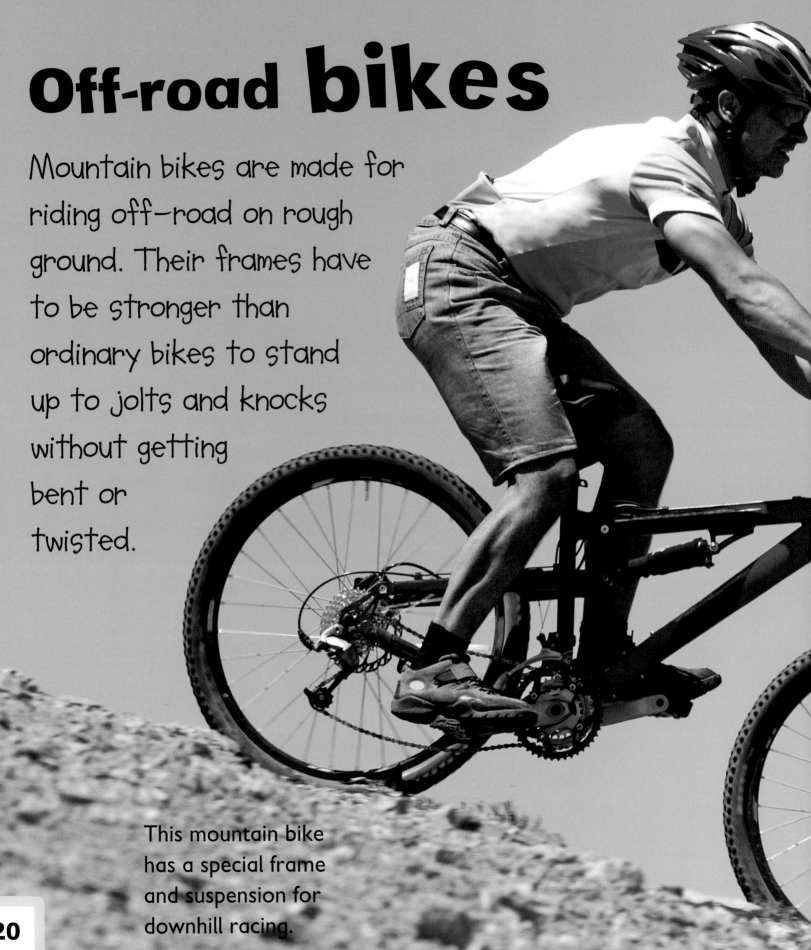

This mountain bike has a special frame and suspension for downhill racing.

A mountain bike can cope with rough forest trails where no ordinary bike can go.

Mountain bikes have fat, bumpy tires and lots of **gears** to make it easier to go up steep hills.

Racing **bikes**

Racing bikes are built for speed. Their tires are so thin, they hardly touch the ground.

Some racing bikes are made specially for long races along roads. Others, called track bikes, are used for indoor races in **velodromes**.

Handcycles are powered by the rider's hands instead of their feet. These racing bikes are popular with disabled riders.

Track bikes often have solid wheels that slip through the air faster than normal wheels with **spokes**.

BMX bikes

BMX stands for Bicycle Motocross.
Riders tear round a circuit of bumps
and jumps on a small-wheeled bike with
a single gear. BMX bikes are made
for racing on hilly dirt tracks and for
freestyle stunt riding.

With their small
frames, fat wheels and
high handlebars, BMX
bikes are great for
doing tricks, such as
wheelies and jumps.

BMX riders need to wear helmets and full protective gear in case of pile-ups.

25

Activities

- Which picture shows a cycle's saddle, handlebars and a gear wheel?

- Make a drawing of your favorite cycle. What sort of cycle is it? Does it have big wheels or small wheels? What color is it?

- Write a story about the cycle ride you would most like to go on. It could be anywhere in the world — or even on another planet! Where would you like to go? Who would you like to meet? What do you think you might see? How long would it take?

- Which of these cycles would a racing cyclist ride?

Cars

What is a **car**?

The job of a car is to carry us from place to place. Every car has an **engine**. The engine burns **fuel** and provides power to turn the wheels.

trunk

The **trunk** in the back of the car is for carrying things.

A car's engine is a complicated machine with hundreds of moving parts. Slippery oil keeps them all moving easily.

hood

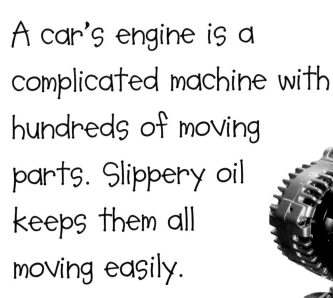

YG06 XPV

In most cars, the engine is at the front, underneath the **hood**.

Everyday **cars**

Cars are made in all shapes and sizes. Small cars, or **compacts**, are good for short journeys. Business people who drive long distances prefer bigger cars with more powerful engines.

A car like this would suit a family with two small children.

All cars need fuel.
The bigger the car,
the more fuel it uses.

To save fuel,
this **hybrid** car is
powered by electric
motors as well as a
gasoline engine.

Sports cars

Sports cars are designed to be fun to drive. They are small, lightweight, **maneuverable** — and fast!

Some sports cars have a top that can be folded down or taken off completely if the weather is fine. This type of car is called a convertible.

The low, smooth shape of this car helps it to go faster by letting air flow easily over it.

The Chevrolet Corvette has one of the biggest engines of any sports car.

Supercars

Supercars are the most powerful sports cars allowed on the roads. Some supercars have engines so big that they are like two ordinary car engines side by side!

air vent

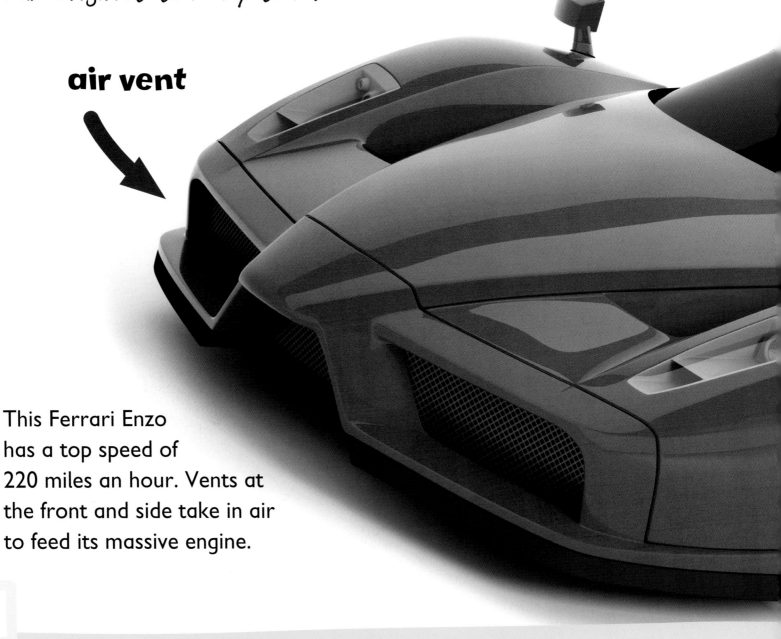

This Ferrari Enzo has a top speed of 220 miles an hour. Vents at the front and side take in air to feed its massive engine.

The Maserati MC12 is built like a racing car, with the engine behind the driver to spread the weight.

Supercars are designed to be the best, whatever the cost. Only a few of these amazing cars are ever built.

On the race track

Motor racing is one of the most **popular** and exciting sports. All sorts of cars can take part. As well as specially built racing cars, there are races for sports cars and even family cars.

These NASCAR cars are the same shape as ordinary cars, but each is a hand-built racer with a top speed of 200 miles an hour.

Top British driver Lewis Hamilton drives a Formula One racing car.

Formula One racing cars are all single-seaters. They are only half the weight of a family car but are ten times more powerful — that's fast!

In the city

City cars that are used mostly for short journeys do not need to be big and powerful. In fact, the smaller they are, the better!

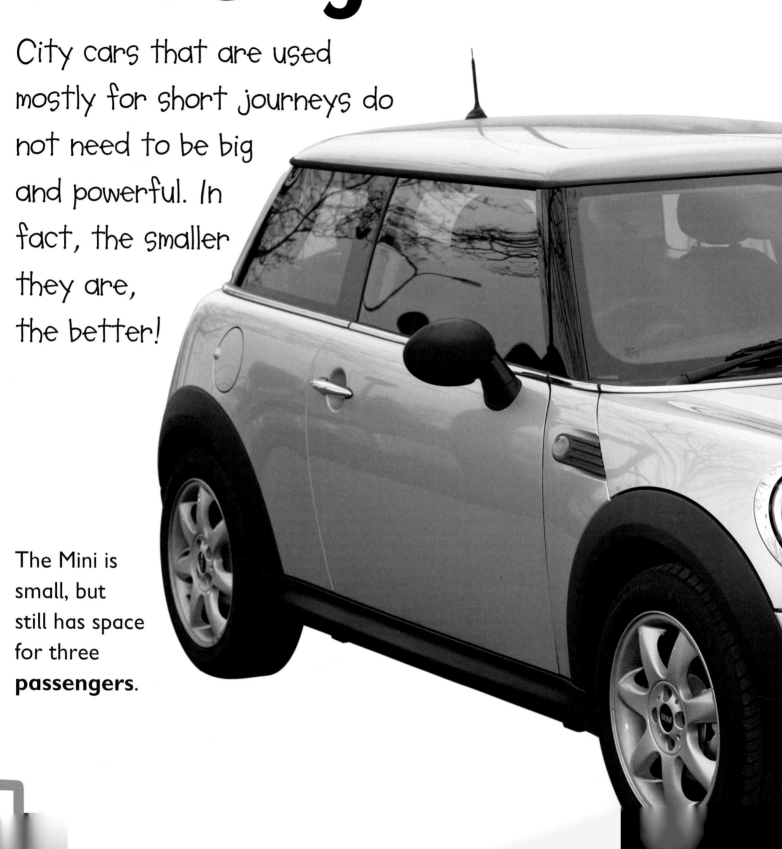

The Mini is small, but still has space for three **passengers**.

In towns and cities, smaller cars are a lot easier to park. They can squeeze into spaces where bigger cars will not fit.

This city car is so short that it can even be parked sideways.

Carrying more

People carriers, or MPVs (multi-purpose **vehicles**), have more space for passengers than ordinary cars.

The seats of an MPV are raised to give the driver and passengers a better view of the road. The back seats fold down easily to make extra carrying space.

This **mini-MPV** is just the right size and shape for carrying emergency medical supplies.

This roomy MPV has eight seats and still has space for the groceries!

Going off-road

When the going gets tough, the car you need is an SUV (Sports Utility Vehicle).

With their chunky tires, SUVs can easily drive over rough or muddy ground without getting stuck. The engine also powers all four wheels, to give more grip on mud, snow and ice.

Only a **four-by-four** could plow through ground as wet and muddy as this!

This Hummer SUV is like the Humvee, the "go-anywhere" patrol car that U.S. Army soldiers drive.

chunky tires

Luxury cars

If you want to travel in real comfort, try a limousine!

Limousines are mostly for important people, such as presidents or kings and queens. But they can be fun to hire for special occasions, such as weddings, too.

The President travels in this specially adapted Cadillac. The body is **armor-plated** and the windows are made of bulletproof glass for protection.

Extra-long luxury cars are called stretch limos. The longest stretch limos have five doors on each side and seats for up to ten passengers!

Rolls-Royce is a famous maker of luxury cars.

45

Activities

- What sort of cars are these?

- Draw your own car and make up a story about it. What sort of car is it? Where is it going, and why? Who is traveling in it?

- Make a collection of pictures of different kinds of cars from magazines and comics. How many types can you find?

- If you had to drive along a muddy road, would a sports car or an SUV be better? Which car would you choose, and why?

- Which of these cars would be driven by a racing driver?

Trains

What is a **train**?

Trains are used to carry people from one place to another. They also carry **goods**, such as cars and coal. A train moves along on tracks.

Some trains carry passengers from one city to another.

At the front of the train is the driver's cab. This is where the driver sits and makes the train start and stop.

Train travel

Trains can travel anywhere there is a track. They can climb mountains and speed across deserts. Trains travel over water using bridges and under water using **tunnels**.

Trains sometimes travel through beautiful countryside.

ROCKY MOUNTAINEER RAILTOURS

In Switzerland, trains travel through mountains covered in snow.

ROCKY MOUNTAINEER RAILTOURS

In some places, trains travel through tunnels that are cut into the mountains. They do this if the mountains are too high or too steep to climb.

Steam trains

The first trains used **steam** to make them move. Steam trains have huge **furnaces** with roaring fires inside. The fire heats water in order to make steam. The steam then powers the engine.

Some steam trains are still in use today. This steam train takes **tourists** along the coast of Namibia, in Africa.

The furnace is at the front of the train. Workers shovel coal into the furnace throughout the journey to keep the train moving.

Keeping the fires burning is a dirty job. It's also a very hot job!

Freight trains

Freight or cargo trains are used to carry different loads from one place to another. It is cheap and fast to transport big, heavy loads by train.

A train with lots of wagons can carry huge loads across the country. The wagons can also make the train very long!

All sorts of goods, such as vegetables, furniture and bricks, are carried by freight trains. Freight trains usually travel a long way.

This freight train is carrying new cars to the car dealer.

Everyday trains

Some trains take people to work in the morning and bring them home again in the evening. These are called **commuter trains**. Commuter trains can get crowded during **rush hour**. Sometimes there are not enough seats for everyone.

Many big cities have underground trains that take people to work and school.

Skytrains

Some trains travel high above the ground. They are called skytrains. These trains move on tracks that are built like a bridge. Skytrains are useful in busy places where there are many people.

Many airports and **amusement parks** have skytrains. They can quickly move people a short distance.

This skytrain is in Detroit, Michigan.
It does not have a driver because
it is controled by a computer.

This skytrain is called a Maglev. It does not have wheels. Instead, it moves using **magnets**.

Water — no problem!

Trains are heavy, so a bridge carrying a train has to be very strong.

Big bridges are built over lakes and rivers so that trains can travel across water. Some bridges have both a road and train tracks. Cars and trains can cross these bridges at the same time.

Some trains travel under the water. They go through special tunnels.

The Channel Tunnel is a long tunnel under the ocean. It connects England to France. Cars can drive onto a special train that takes them through the tunnel.

Express trains

Some trains quickly carry passengers long distances. These are called express trains. They stop at only a few stations and travel very fast.

This tilting train travels very fast.

Some express trains can **tilt** slightly as they go around **curves** in the track. This is so they do not have to slow down.

Some trains have huge windows and a glass roof. Passengers can enjoy the view as they travel!

Sleeper cars

Some passenger trains have to travel long distances through the night. These trains have special **cars** called sleeper cars. In sleeper cars, passengers can sleep and even take a shower in the morning!

These kinds of trains also have a restaurant on board where people can eat.

Some train trips last for many days, so it is important to have a comfortable bed.

Activities

- Collect train pictures from magazines. Put them in a book or on the wall in groups, such as: trains that carry people, steam trains or trains crossing a bridge.

- Look at this train. Do you think this is a steam train? Why?

- Make up a story about a train. What kind of train is it? Where is it going? What is it carrying? What happens during the trip?

- Have you been on a train recently? Where were you going? Who were you with? Did you enjoy it? Was the train fast or slow? Full or empty? Draw a picture of yourself on the train.

- Look at these three pictures. Which one shows train tracks?

  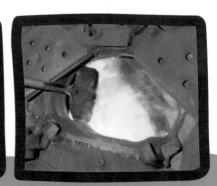

Tractors
AND FARM VEHICLES

What is a **tractor?**

cab

The cab has large windows so the driver can see what is happening.

This tractor is pulling a heavy trailer across a field.

Tractors are big machines that are used mostly on farms. They help farmers prepare their land and plant, care for and **harvest** their crops.

A tractor has a **cab**. The driver sits in the cab. Other machines can be hooked onto the back of a tractor, so it can do many different jobs.

Watch those wheels!

A tractor has big wheels, so it can travel across bumpy fields. The huge wheels also help stop the tractor from sinking into mud.

Some tractors have two or even three sets of wheels on each side.

Tractor wheels are made to grip soft, muddy ground.

Preparing the fields

Farmers need to prepare their fields before they can plant **crops**. To do this, farmers attach a **plow** to the back of a tractor.

A plow is a long row of metal blades. The blades turn as they are pulled through the ground.

72

The plow has sharp **blades** that cut through the dirt. The tractor pulls the plow through the fields. The plow blades chop up the dirt and turn it over. The plow makes rows of ditches, or **furrows**.

Sowing the seeds

When the fields are prepared, farmers plant, or sow, seeds. They do this with a seed drill. A seed drill is a container, or row of containers, that is attached to the back of a tractor. The containers are filled with seeds.

This seed drill is being filled with corn seeds.

As the seed drill is pulled across the fields by the tractor, seeds are dropped into the furrows in the ground.

The seed drill plants the seeds in straight rows.

Taking care of crops

Once they start growing, the new crops need to be cared for. Some farmers spray their crops with a special liquid. The liquid stops bugs from eating the plants. The liquid also stops weeds from growing.

Some farmers do not spray their crops. Instead, workers remove weeds with their hands as they are pulled through the fields.

A machine called a crop sprayer can be hooked to the back of a tractor. As the tractor moves through the fields, liquid is sprayed on the growing crops.

A crop sprayer has long arms on each side. The liquid sprays out of these arms.

Harvest time

When crops are fully grown, they must be harvested. Different machines are used to harvest different crops. Vegetable harvesters dig up vegetables that grow under the ground.

The green tractor is pulling a machine that harvests potatoes.

Vegetable harvesters pull vegetables out of the ground. Then the vegetables are dropped into a truck.

Some harvesters can dig up two rows of carrots at a time.

Collecting wheat

Wheat is ready to harvest when it is tall and **ripe**. This is done with a machine called a combine harvester. The front of a combine harvester has sharp blades that spin around.

Many combine harvesters work together to harvest large fields.

As the blades of a combine harvester spin, they cut the long stalks of wheat.

The wheat is sucked into the harvester. The grain of the wheat is separated from its stalk inside the harvester.

81

Baling hay

After a field of wheat has been harvested, the cut stalks are left behind — this is called hay. A special machine called a baler cuts the hay and makes it into round or square **bales**.

The bales of hay are tied up tightly and dropped out of the baler.

A tractor loads the bales of hay onto a trailer. The bales are then taken away to be stored.

The hay is used as food for farm animals. During the winter, hay is also used as bedding for the animals.

Pull, tractor!

Tractors can be used for work — and for play! Tractor pulls are very exciting. People watch tractor pulls to see which tractor will pull the heaviest weight.

The tractors race on a special **track**. They have huge back wheels to stop them from slipping. The tractors pull a heavy load behind them while the crowd cheers.

During a pull, a tractor's front wheels may lift off the ground.

Activities

- Would you like to be a farmer who drives a big tractor? Would it be fun? Would it be hard work? Draw a picture of yourself driving a tractor.

- Here are two tractors you have seen in this book. Can you remember what jobs they do?

- Write a story about a runaway tractor. How will your story start? Who will be in your story? What happens at the end? Can you draw a picture to go with your story?

- Look through the book again. Write a list of jobs that are done on the farm and the machines you need to do them. How many different machines are needed? Which job do you think would be your favorite? Why?

Fire Trucks
AND RESCUE VEHICLES

Quick! Emergency!

If there is an accident or if someone is in trouble, an emergency vehicle and specially trained people rush to the scene to help.

Whenever there is a traffic accident or emergency, the police come to help out.

Fire engines, ambulances, police cars, lifeboats and rescue helicopters are all emergency vehicles. Most emergency cars and trucks have a **siren** and flashing lights. These let people know to clear the way for emergency vehicles when they are racing through traffic.

Help! Fire!

Fire engines and fire trucks arrive quickly to put out a fire. Fire engines have tanks of water with hoses that are used to pour water onto the fire. Fire trucks have long ladders that are used to rescue people from high buildings. Firefighters wear special uniforms and helmets to protect them from the smoke and the heat of the flames.

Fire trucks have metal arms at the side. This is to stop the truck from tipping over when the ladder is being used.

Fire truck ladders can be turned in all directions to reach people trapped in fires.

Forest **fires**

In some countries, forest fires start when the weather is very hot and dry. Special airplanes and helicopters are used to put out these fires. A tank full of water is carried underneath the airplane or helicopter. **Pilots** can open the water tank using special controls.

As this Firehawk helicopter flies over the forest, it drops water onto the fire below.

Helicopters are also used to rescue people or animals from hard-to-reach places. This is a mountain rescue helicopter carrying a dog to safety.

Airport accidents

Special equipment is needed to fight fires in airports. This is because airplanes are very big. It's also because airports and airplanes are usually filled with hundreds of people.

Airport fire trucks are built to put out a fire on an airplane and rescue any passengers trapped on board the plane.

This airport truck has special lights at the front to see through thick smoke.

Harbor **Firefighter**

The **harbor** in New York City is used by hundreds of people every day. If a fire starts, the New York City Fire Department has a special boat called *Firefighter* that goes to the rescue.

The boat carries extra-long hoses and big water tanks to put out fires quickly and stop them from spreading.

Fireboats can pump a lot of water onto a fire and can rescue both people and goods.

Other harbors have fireboats, too. They put out fires on ships and rescue passengers.

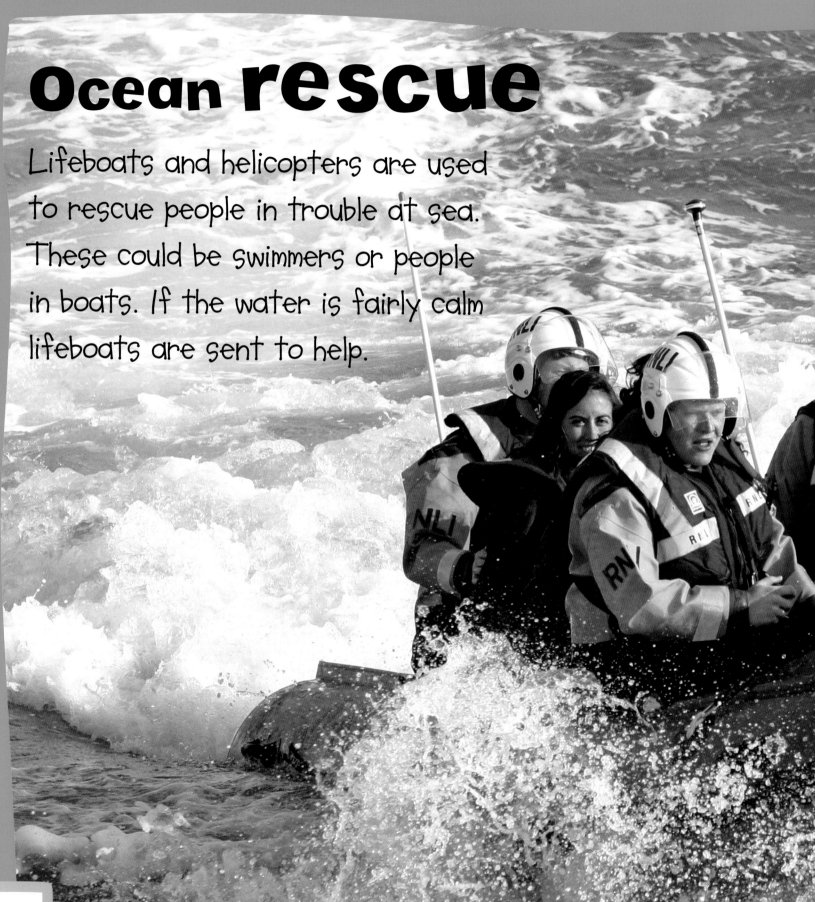

Ocean rescue

Lifeboats and helicopters are used to rescue people in trouble at sea. These could be swimmers or people in boats. If the water is fairly calm lifeboats are sent to help.

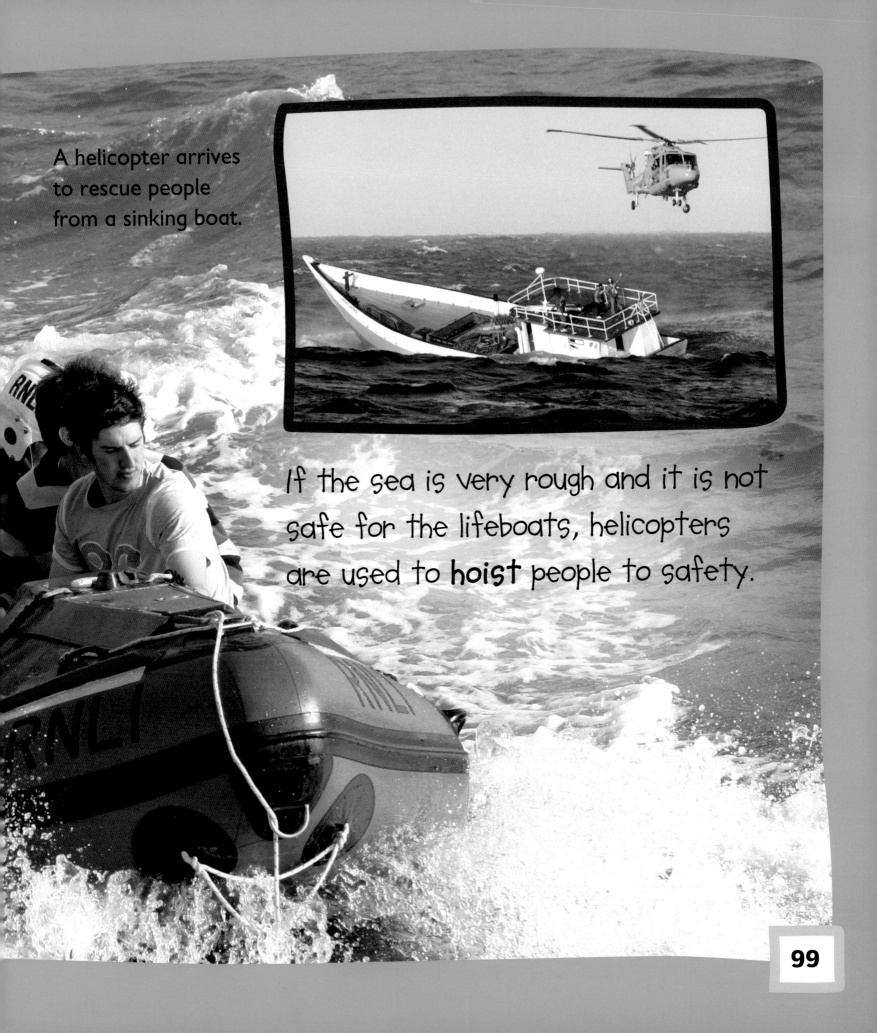

A helicopter arrives to rescue people from a sinking boat.

If the sea is very rough and it is not safe for the lifeboats, helicopters are used to **hoist** people to safety.

Send an **ambulance!**

If someone has been badly **injured** or suddenly becomes very ill, an ambulance is called. The ambulance puts on its flashing lights and loud siren and rushes to help the person, or take the person to the hospital.

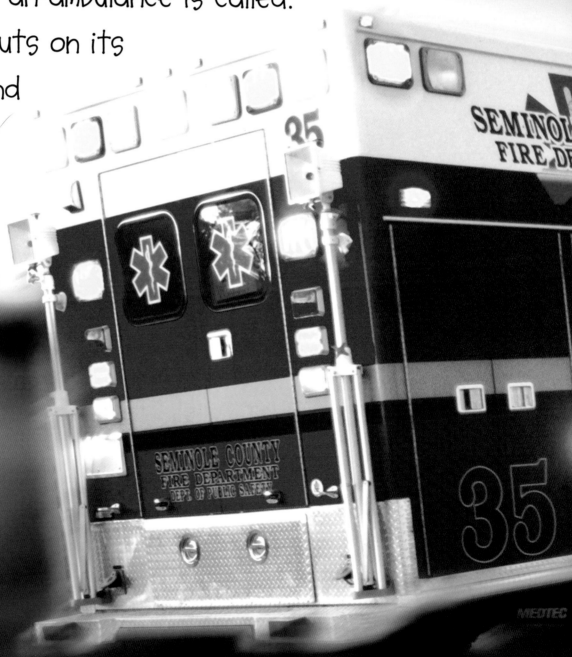

Inside the back of an ambulance is a bed, medical equipment, and somewhere for the **paramedics** to sit.

Some places are difficult to reach by road. An air ambulance helicopter is used instead.

Paramedics are people trained to care for the sick or injured person inside the ambulance.

Police on the way!

Police cars can race to the scene of a crime or accident. Police drivers have been trained to drive at high speeds on busy roads and highways.

Police cars have computers that allow officers to check information, such as if a car is stolen or not.

Sometimes a police helicopter is used to chase people on the roads who are speeding, or **criminals** who are trying to escape.

Motorcycle patrol

In very crowded cities, some police use motorcycles to help them reach an accident quickly or chase criminals through busy streets.

Sometimes motorcycle police travel with the cars of important people in order to keep them safe.

Motorcycle police always wear safety helmets and they have to be specially trained to ride their bikes.

Activities

- Start your own collection of emergency vehicle pictures. Group them together, for example ambulances, fire engines, police cars and so on. Which are your favorites? Why?

- Do you know what each of these emergency vehicles is used for? What can you see in each picture?

- On a big sheet of paper, draw your favorite emergency vehicle. Then imagine there is a telephone call. There has been an accident. Quick, you must help! Make up a story about what happens next.

- Which vehicle does a police officer drive?

Dump Trucks

AND OTHER BIG MACHINES

What is a dump truck?

Dump **trucks**, diggers, loaders and bulldozers are all types of **construction** vehicles. These big machines help to build roads, bridges, tunnels and tall buildings.

Some construction vehicles carry materials for building. Others have tools for digging, lifting and pushing.

These two diggers are being carried to work on the back of a transporter.

The huge back section of this dump truck can carry up to 150 tons of dirt and rubble.

Diggers

Digging machines, or excavators, work by pushing a metal **bucket** into the ground so that it fills up with dirt.

digging bucket

In one day, the biggest excavator in the world can dig a hole that is 60 feet deep!

Big metal teeth on the front of the digging bucket help to break up the ground.

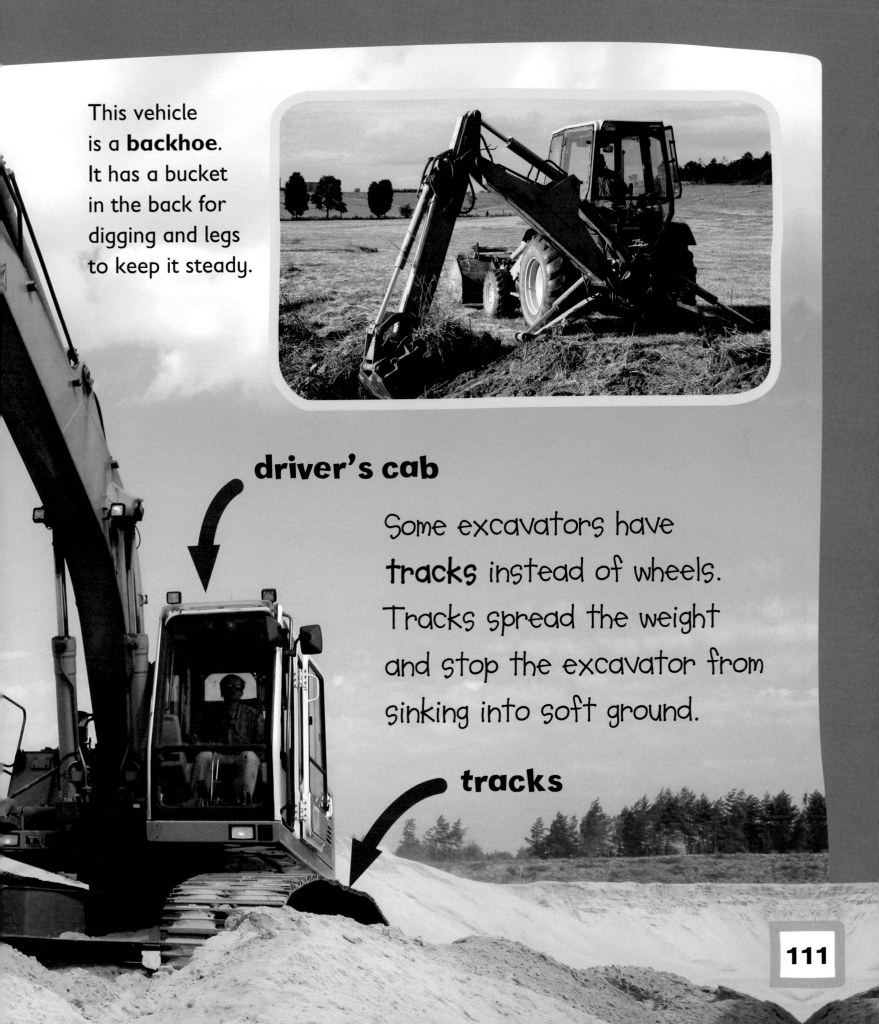

This vehicle is a **backhoe**. It has a bucket in the back for digging and legs to keep it steady.

driver's cab

Some excavators have **tracks** instead of wheels. Tracks spread the weight and stop the excavator from sinking into soft ground.

tracks

Trucks

Before building work can begin on a **construction site**, huge piles of dirt and rubble may need to be shifted. Dump trucks and tipper trucks do this work.

Big trucks also deliver sand, gravel, bricks and other building materials to the construction site.

A tipper truck tips up at the back to empty its load onto the ground.

Dump trucks

Some of the world's biggest
trucks are dump trucks.
These trucks are used to move
earth and rocks where **mines**
are being dug.

Dump trucks have
huge wheels, more
than three times
taller than you.

This dump truck is emptying its load backward. With some dump trucks, no one has to do any **manual** unloading.

Smaller dump trucks are used on construction sites. The back of the truck tips up so that the load slides off.

Loaders

It would take a long time to fill a dump truck by hand! A machine called a loader can do the job much more quickly.

Smaller loaders are useful for working in awkward spaces.

A loader scoops up dirt in a big, wide bucket. Then the bucket is lifted up over a truck and the dirt is tipped into it.

As well as filling trucks, a front loader's powerful arms can push dirt and rubble along the ground like a bulldozer.

Concrete mixers

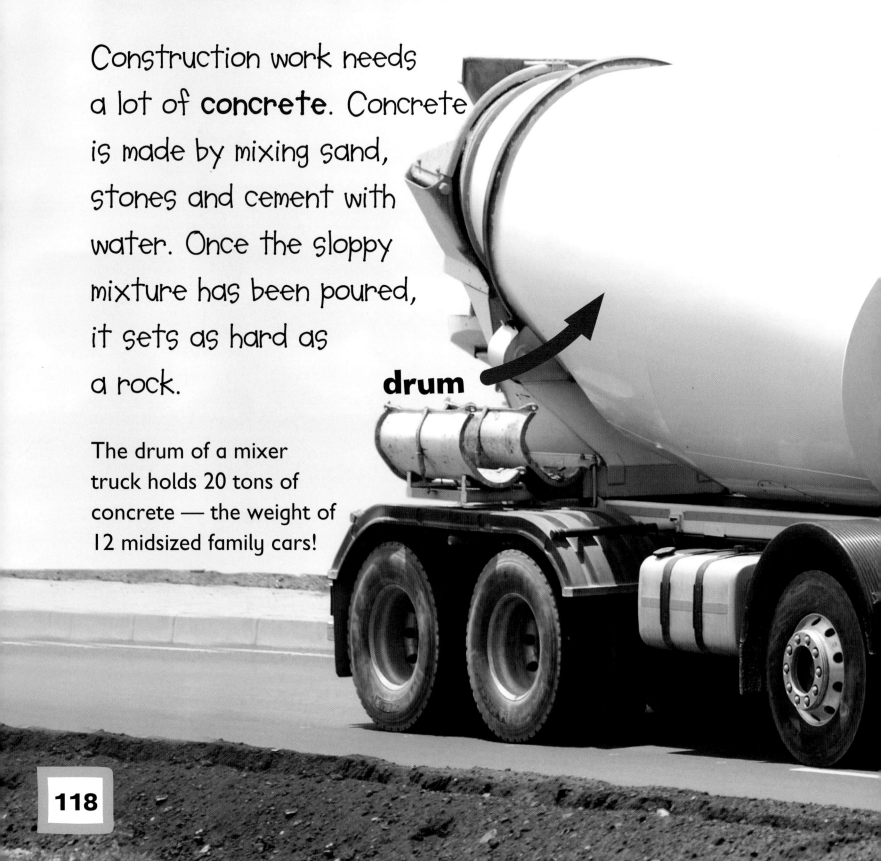

Construction work needs a lot of **concrete**. Concrete is made by mixing sand, stones and cement with water. Once the sloppy mixture has been poured, it sets as hard as a rock.

drum

The drum of a mixer truck holds 20 tons of concrete — the weight of 12 midsized family cars!

118

Concrete is brought to construction sites by mixer trucks. The concrete is carried in a big drum, which keeps turning to stop the cement from setting hard.

chute

On this mixer truck, the drum is emptied by pouring the concrete down a chute in the back.

Bulldozers

Bulldozers are big, powerful machines that are used to move dirt and rubble. A blade at the front of a bulldozer scrapes up the dirt and pushes it along in front.

blade

Bulldozers are used to clear the land to make it ready for building. They can flatten a big area very quickly.

Tracks help a bulldozer to grip the ground, so they can push hard.

tracks

Cranes on wheels

If a tall building is being constructed, materials and other heavy loads may have to be lifted high above the ground.

The **boom** is lowered when the crane is moving.

boom

122

On big construction sites, tall cranes are kept busy all the time. On smaller sites, special **mobile** cranes are brought in when they are needed.

Strong legs called **outriggers** stop the crane from tipping over.

outrigger

123

Roadbuilders

Before a road can be built, the ground has to be made very flat. Bulldozers and machines called scrapers and graders are used to flatten the area.

A grader scrapes a blade along the ground to smooth out the bumps.

Then vehicles called pavement-layers, or pavers, can get to work.

To make the surface of a road, a pavement-layer uses a mixture of stones and hot, sticky **tar**.

blade

Tunnelers

If a road or railroad has to cross a river or a hill, the quickest way is often to dig a tunnel under it.

Long, underground tunnels are made by tunnel-boring machines. These rock-eating monsters cut their way through solid rock like long, metal worms.

A tunnel-boring machine can carve out 65 feet of finished tunnel a day.

The huge cutting head of this tunnel borer spins around to cut through rock and dirt.

cutting head

Long trucks

Long trucks, called **tandem-trailer trucks**, carry loads over very long distances. Some drivers spend months on the road, so their trucks have beds, refrigerators, toilets and even televisions inside.

Tandem-trailer trucks pull huge trailers. Each trailer can be as long as ten cars lined up in a row.

Each trailer has several sets of chunky wheels.

Logging trucks

When trees are cut down,
trucks called loggers
are used to carry
the logs to the
timber mills.

A stack of logs is loaded onto the long trailer behind the logging truck's cab.

Loggers often have to travel long distances to timber mills.

Activities

- Here are two construction vehicles from the book. Can you remember which jobs they do?

- If you had to build a house, which construction vehicles would you need, and why?

- Make a drawing of your favorite construction vehicle. What sort of vehicle is it? What color is it? Where is it? What is it doing? Who is driving it?

- Which of these pictures shows an excavator?

Monster Trucks

What are monster trucks?

Monster trucks are the world's biggest, fastest and most powerful trucks.

Monster trucks with extra-large wheels thrill the crowds at truck shows, while other giant trucks move the biggest and heaviest loads.

When a huge load has to be moved by road, only a giant truck can do the job.

Monster trucks often have tires as tall as a normal-sized car!

tire

Bigfoot
monster trucks

The world's first monster truck was Bigfoot 1. It was built in 1975 from an ordinary **pick-up truck,** but special wheels and parts were added to make it bigger and better.

After Bigfoot 1, lots more Bigfoot monster trucks were built.

The wheels of Bigfoot trucks are so huge that children can easily stand inside them!

Bigfoot Fastrax is different from the other Bigfoots because it has tank tracks instead of wheels.

Car crushers

Car crushing is a favorite event in monster truck shows. The trucks drive over the top of scrap cars and squash them flat.

With their huge weight and powerful wheels, monster trucks make short work of flattening cars.

To make car crushing safe, car **batteries**, fuel and glass must be removed first. Drivers must also wear fireproof suits and crash helmets.

How would YOU like a ride in this champion car crusher?

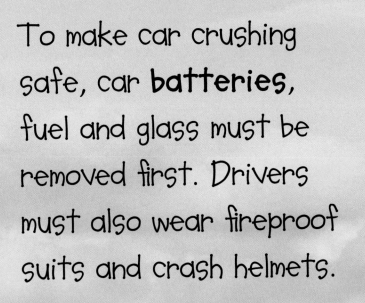

Monster **racers**

Races between monster trucks are held in **stadiums**, on race tracks and on closed roads. In a hill climb, the trucks race up a dirt track to the top of a hill.

Not all racing trucks are giant-sized. Some are ordinary road trucks. Others are built specially for racing on **circuits**.

A powerful rally truck roars around a bend in a twisting hill-climb race.

Big crowds turn out to watch their favorite trucks compete in races and other stadium events.

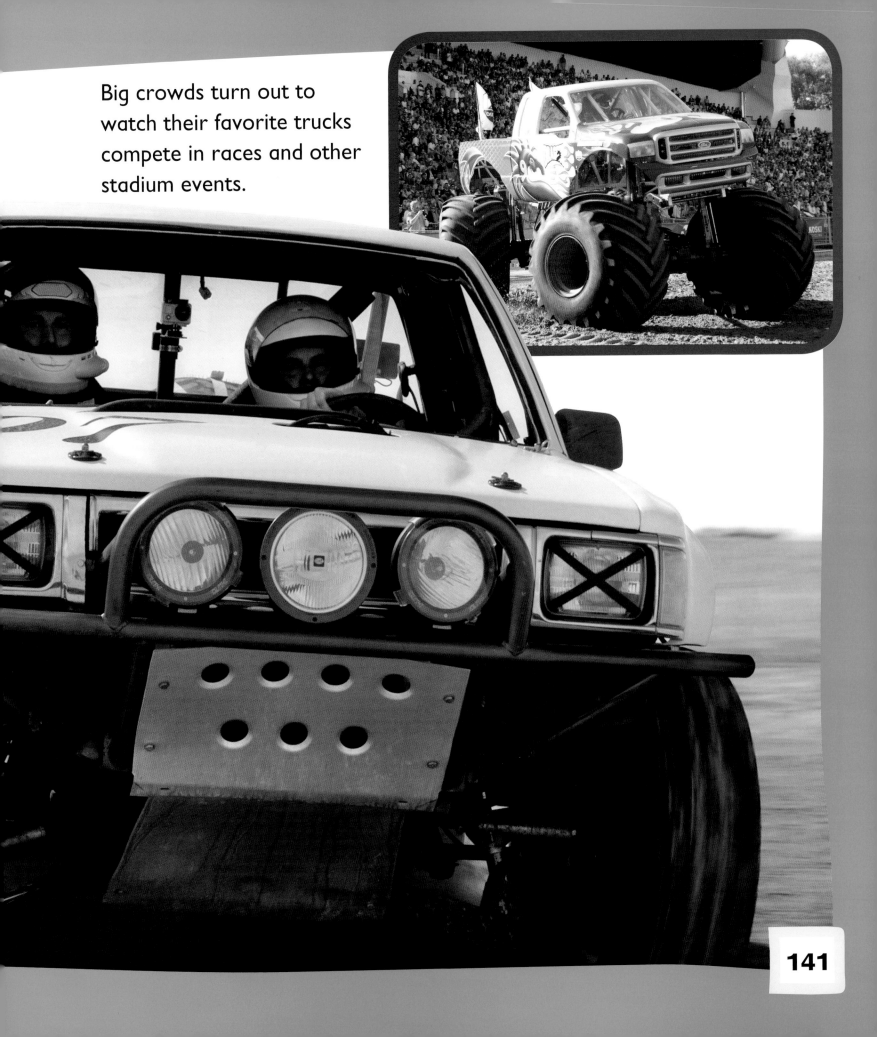

Truck **stunts** and **tricks**

In the **freestyle** part of a monster truck show, drivers make their trucks do amazing tricks and stunts.

The crowds love to see the trucks jump into the air, ride over ramps, do wheelies and spin around on end!

The roof of a monster truck must be strong to protect the driver if the truck turns over.

A monster truck jumps into the air during a freestyle competition.

LUCAS OIL

Monster **stars**

The leading monster trucks are as famous as pop stars. Each one has a different name and is painted in its own special style.

Jurassic Attack is painted to look like a dinosaur's head.

Fans of the trucks cheer them on as they battle it out in competitions and races.

Samson's bulging muscles look as if they mean business!

Road giants

While monster trucks and car crushers entertain the crowds, hardworking giant trucks **haul** some of the biggest, heaviest and longest loads ever carried on wheels.

The part of the truck that does the pulling is called the tractor. Behind it, the trailer carries the load.

Imagine seeing a whole house coming toward you along the road!

This huge trailer is carrying parts of an Airbus A380 — the biggest aircraft ever built!

tractor

trailer

Monster miners

The biggest trucks in the world are called dump trucks. Their job is to haul huge loads of rock dug from under the ground. The rock often contains valuable metals, such as copper.

These trucks can never leave the mines where they work, because they are far too big to go on ordinary roads.

The biggest dump trucks are so huge that the driver has to climb a set of steps to reach the cab.

Giant dump trucks
need even bigger
machines to
load them.

NASA's giants

The space agency NASA has two giant vehicles to transport its huge space shuttle craft to the **launch pad**. These two monsters are called crawler-transporters.

tracks

Each crawler-transporter runs on eight **tracks** powered by electric motors.

space shuttle

The crawler-transporters were first built in the 1960s. At that time they were the biggest tracked vehicles ever made.

Because of their size, crawler-transporters can only move at a snail's pace. This huge vehicle weighs 2,870 tons and carries around 5,000 gallons of fuel.

Activities

- Which of these trucks is doing a wheelie?

- Make a drawing of your own monster truck with extra-big wheels. Think of a name for it and then color it to suit its name.

- Look at these pictures. Which one is a dump truck?

- Can you remember what NASA's giant crawler-transporters carry?

Glossary

Amusement parks Parks with rides, games and vendors.

Armor-plated Specially strengthened to protect against bullets or missiles.

Backhoe A digging machine that works by pulling a bucket through the ground.

Bales Large bundles of cut hay that are tied up very tightly.

Battery The part that supplies electricity to a car or truck.

Blades Sharp, flat pieces of metal used for cutting.

Boom The main arm of a crane, which is also called the jib.

Bucket The part of a digging machine that scoops dirt out of the ground.

Cab The place where the tractor driver sits and uses the controls to move the machine.

Cargo Items carried from one place to another by train. Also called freight.

Cars The parts of a train where the passengers sit.

Chrome A shiny coating on metal.

Circuit A track built specially for racing.

Commuter trains Trains that take people to and from their place of work.

Compact A type of car suitable for a small family.

Concrete A mixture of sand, stones, cement, and water that sets hard. It is used to make buildings.

Construction Another word for building.

Construction site An area of land where buildings, such as houses or offices, are built.

Crawler-transporter A vehicle that runs on tracks for moving very large or heavy loads.

Criminals People who have broken the law by doing something such as stealing.

Crops Plants that farmers grow, such as vegetables or wheat.

Glossary

Curves Lines that bend.

Customize To alter or add to something to make it special for the owner.

Engine The machine inside a car that provides power to make the wheels go round.

Exhaust A pipe that carries waste gases away from the engine of a cycle.

Four-by-four A car in which the engine drives all four wheels, not just the two in the front or back.

Freestyle Part of a monster truck show where drivers do tricks and stunts.

Freight Items carried from one place to another by train. Also called cargo.

Fuel The liquid burned inside a car engine to make it go. Most car engines burn gasoline or diesel.

Furnaces The places where fire burns to make steam for the train's engine.

Furrows Long, narrow cuts in the ground made by a plow.

Gear A toothed wheel that lets the pedals turn the wheels of a cycle at different speeds.

Goods Things such as clothes, food, cars or books. They can be moved by boat, plane, train or truck.

Grain The part of the wheat that is used to make flour for bread. Grains are like tiny seeds.

Harbor A safe place where ships and boats can stay. This is where boats unload and collect their goods and where passenger boats pick up and drop off people.

Harvest To cut and collect all the crops that are fully grown or ripe.

Haul To transport or carry by truck.

Hoist To pull someone on board a plane or helicopter using a rope.

Hood The part of a car's body at the front that protects the engine.

Hybrid A car that saves fuel by using electric motors as well as a gasoline engine to drive the wheels.

Glossary

Injured   When someone has been hurt.

Launch pad   The platform from which a rocket takes off.

Loads   A large amount of something that is carried from one place to another.

Magnets   Magnets use an invisible force to pull metal things toward them or push metal things away from them. This force is called magnetism.

Maneuverable   Easy to steer or control.

Manual   A process carried out by hand.

Mines   A place where things such as coal or gold are dug out of the ground.

Mini-MPV   An MPV with fewer seats but a tall space behind for carrying things.

Mobile   Able to move from place to place.

Obstacle   Something that is placed in the way of a cycle to slow it down.

Outrigger   A part that sticks out from the side of a construction machine to make it steadier or stop it from tipping over.

Paramedics   The men and women who drive the ambulance and care for injured people until they reach the hospital.

Passengers   People who travel inside a car, bus, train, boat or airplane.

Pick-up truck   A light truck with low sides.

Pilots   The people who fly planes and helicopters.

Plow   A machine that breaks up the dirt and prepares it for seeds to be planted.

Popular   Liked by a lot of people.

Ripe   Crops that are fully grown and ready to harvest.

Rush hour   Time of the day when large numbers of people travel to and from work.

Siren   A loud noise used by emergency vehicles when they are traveling very fast. It's used to warn other vehicles on the road that an emergency vehicle is coming through.

Spokes   Thin, metal wires that connect the center of a bicycle wheel with the edge.

Glossary

Stadium A sports ground with seats where people watch races and other events.

Steam Clouds of gas that come from boiling water.

Suspension A set of springs that connects a cycle's wheels and frame to give a smoother ride. The springs let the wheels follow bumps in the ground, while the rest of the cycle moves along smoothly.

Tandem-trailer trucks Really big, long trucks that can pull up to six trailers.

Tar A thick, black, oily, sticky liquid used to make the surface of a road.

Tilt When something leans to one side.

Timber mills A place where large logs are cut into smaller pieces.

Tire A rubber tube filled with air that fits around the edge of a wheel.

Tourist Someone who travels for pleasure.

Track A special path where tractors race.

Tracks Metal belts used by bulldozers and some other construction vehicles instead of wheels to spread the weight and stop them from sinking into soft ground.

Traffic Cars, trucks, buses, and other vehicles that use the roads.

Trail A dirt track for riding motorcycles off-road.

Truck A big road or construction vehicle used for moving heavy loads.

Trunk Space in the back of a car for carrying things.

Tunnels Underground passageways for trains.

Vehicle A machine with an engine that carries people or things.

Velodrome A race track specially designed for cycle racing.

Wheelies When a truck stands up or drives along on just its back wheels.

Index

Index

Index

Index